# ŠEVČÍK

## OPUS 2 PART 2

SCHOOL OF BOWING
TECHNIQUE

SCHULE DER
BOGENTECHNIK

ÉCOLE DU MÉCANISME
DE L'ARCHET

for

# CELLO

ARR. FEUILLARD

BOSWORTH

(Heft II). | (Cahier II). | (Section II.)

*ODDĚLENÍ PRVNÍ. (Seš. II.)* | ЦЕРВАЯ ЧАСТЬ. (Тетрадь II)

# № 13.

| | | |
|---|---|---|
| Etude in Triolen mit 105 Veränderungen des Bogenstriches. | Etude en triolets avec 105 changements de coups d'archet. | Studies in Triplets with 105 changes of style in bowing. |
| Dieselbe in den Daumenlagen, siehe № 26. | La même aux positions du pouce, voir № 26. | The same in the Positions of the Thumb, see № 26. |
| | *Cvičení triolové se 105 proměnami smyku.* | Этюдъ тріолями съ 105 перемѣнами движенія смычка. |
| | *Totéž v poloze palcové (viz čís 26)* | Тоже самое въ позиціяхъ большого пальца. См. № 26. |

Edited and translated by H. Brett.

Edited by L. R. Feuillard and A. E. Bosworth.

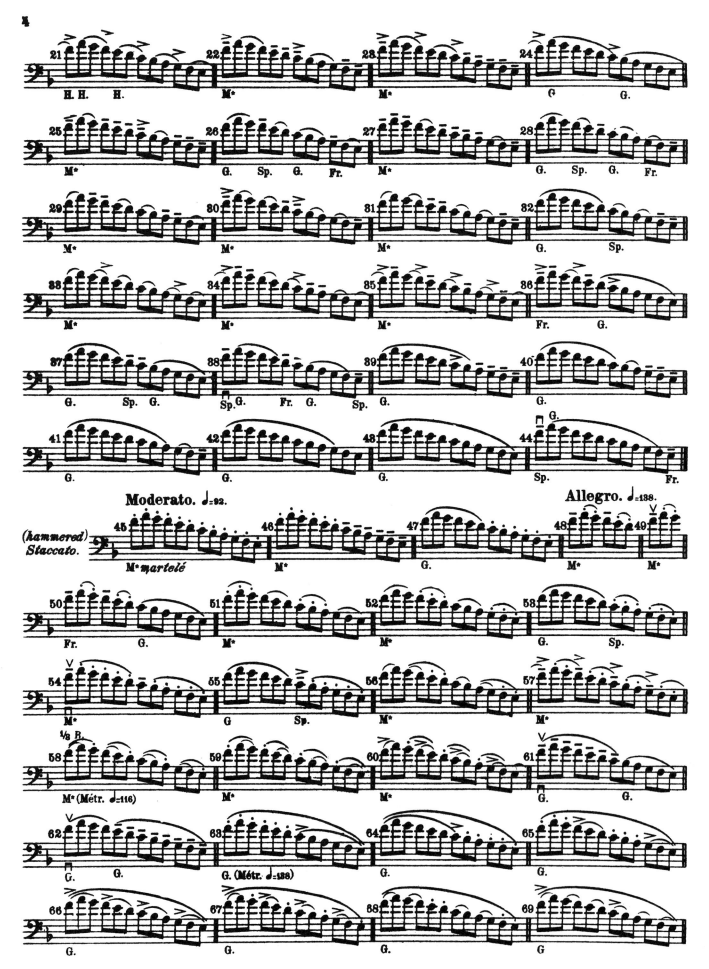

**6**

# № 14.

Etude in Triolen (¾ Takt) mit 77
Veränderungen des Bogenstriches.
Dieselbe in den Daumenlagen, siehe № 25.

Etude en triolets (mesure ¾) avec 77
changements de coups d'archet.
La même aux positions du pouce, voir
№ 25.

*Cvičení triolové (¾ takt) se 77 promě-
nami smyku.*
*Totéž v poloze palcové, viz čís 25.*

Study in Triplets (¾-time) with 77
changes of style in bowing.
The same in the Positions of the Thumb, see
№ 25.

Этюдъ тріолями (въ ¾ тактѣ) съ 77
перемѣнами движенія смычка.
Тоже самое въ позиціяхъ большого пальца. См. № 25.

Allegro.

*f*

*decresc.* *p*

pizz.

Stricharten.
*Coups d'archet.*
Bowing-styles.

*Druhy smyku.*
Движенія см.

(Métr. ♩=100)
1 · 2 · 8 · 4 ·
M⁺  M⁺  G. Sp.  Fr.  G. Sp.

5 · 6 · 7 · 8 · 9
G.  G.  G.  G.  G.  G.  G.  G.  G

10 · 11 · 12 · 13 · 14
Fr.  G.  G.  G.  G.  G.

(Métr. ♩=112, ♩=126, ♩=144)
15 · 16 · 17 · 18 · 19
M⁺  G.  Sp.  M⁺  M⁺  G.  Sp.

B. & Cº 6125

# № 15.

Etude in Sechzehnteln (6/8 Takt) mit 64 Veränderungen des Bogenstriches.
Dieselbe in den Daumenlagen, siehe № 27.

Etude en doubles croches (mesure 6/8) avec 64 changements de coups d'archet.
La même aux positions du pouce, voir. № 27.

Cvičení v šestnáctinách (6/8 takt) se 64 proměnami smyku.
Totéž v poloze palcové, viz č. 27.

Study in semiquavers (16th notes) (in 6/8-measure) with 64 changes of style in bowing.
The same in the Positions of the Thumb, see № 27

Этюдъ шестнадцатыми (въ 6/8 тактѣ) съ 64 перемѣнами движенія смычка.
Тоже самое въ позиціяхъ большого пальца. См. № 27.

Allegro moderato.

Stricharten.
Coups d'archet.
Bowing-styles.

Druhy smyku.
Движенія см.

# № 16.

Etude in Sechzehnteln (3/4 Takt) mit 68 Veränderungen des Bogenstriches.

Etude en doubles croches (mesure 3/4) avec 68 changements de coups d'archet.

*Cvičení v šestnáctinách (3/4 takt) s 68 proměnami smyku*

Study in semiquavers (16th notes, –in 6/8 time) with 68 changes of style in bowing.

Этюдъ шестнадцатыми (въ 3/4 тактѣ) съ 68 перемѣнами движенія смычка.

B. & Cᵒ 6125

# № 17.

Etude in Sechzehnteln (⁴⁄₄ Takt) mit
131 Veränderungen des Bogenstriches.
Dieselbe mit Daumenlagen, siehe № 28.

Etude en doubles croches (mesure ⁴⁄₄)
avec 181 changements de coups d'archet.
La même avec positions du pouce, voir № 28.

*Cvičení v šestnáctinách ( ⁴⁄₄ takt) se
131 proměnami smyku.*
*Totéž v poloze palcové, viz. č. 28.*

Study in semiquavers (16th notes, - in
⁴⁄₄, - or common time) with 131 changes
of style in bowing.
The same with Positions of the Thumb, see № 28.

Этюдъ шестнадцатыми ( въ ⁴⁄₄ тактѣ)
съ 131 перемѣнами движенія смычка.
Тоже самое въ позиціяхъ большого пальца;
См. № 28.

Stricharten.
*Coups d'archet.*
Bowing - styles.

*Druhy smyku.*
Движенія см.

*) Die zweite Takthälfte ebenso wie die erste.

*) La seconde moitié de la mesure de même que la
première.
*) Druha polovice taktu jako prvni.

*) The second half of each bar exactly like the first.
*) Вторую половину такта точно также какъ первую.

B. & C⁰ 6125

Punktierte Sechzehntel.
*Doubles croches pointées.*
Dotted semiquavers (16th notes.)

*Tečkované šestnáctiny.*
Шестнадцатыя съ точкой.

Moderato. ♩ = 100.

*Spiccato.*

Uebungen im *pp* am Griffbrett für die Ausbildung der Weichheit des Tones.

Exercices en *pp* sur la touche pour développer la douceur du son.
*Cvičení v pp. na hmatníku za příčinou dosažení měkkého tonu.*

Exercises in *pp* on the finger-board, for the development of softness of tone.

Упражненія въ *pp* на грифѣ для выработки мягкости тона.

## № 18.

Beispiel mit 30 Varianten.

Exemple avec 30 variantes.
*Příklad s 30 proměnami.*

Example with 30 Variations.

Примѣръ съ 30 варіантами.

Varianten.

Variantes.
*Obměny.*

Variations.

Варіанты.

Mit halbem Bogen.
*Moitié de l'archet.*
With the half bow-length.
*Polovicí smyčce.*
Половиною смычка.

Mit halbem und ganzem Bogen.
*Moitié de l'archet et tout l'archet.*
With half and whole bow length.
*Polovičním a celým smyčcem.*
Половиною и цѣлымъ смычкомъ.

Mit der Mitte.
*Du milieu.*
In the middle (of the bow)
*Středem.*
Серединою.

## № 19.

Fortsetzung der Uebungen im *pp* am Griffbrett.
Etude mit 59 Varianten.

Suite des exercices en *pp* sur la touche.
Etude avec 59 variantes.
*Pokračování ve cvičeních v pp na hmatníku.*
*Cvičení s 59 proměnami.*

Continuation of the exercises in *pp* on the finger-board. Study with 59 Variations.
Продолженіе упражненій въ *pp* на грифѣ.
Этюдъ съ 59 варіантами.

Moderato. ♩ = 80.

sempre *pp* sulla tastiera

restez

Varianten.
*Variantes.*
Variations.
*Proměny.*
Варіанты.

# № 20.

Uebung in gehaltenen Tönen und im Zurückhalten des Bogens.
Die vorhergehenden Etuden № 3 – 7 und 13 – 17 sind auf folgende Arten zu üben:

a) zu 2 Takten unter einem Bogenstrich im *f*
b) zu 4 Takten unter einem Bogenstrich im *p*
c) zu 8 Takten unter einem Bogenstrich im *ppp*

Exercice des sons filés et de la retenue d'archet.
On travaillera les études précédentes № 3 – 7 et 13 – 17 en liant les mesures des manières suivantes:

a) par 2 mesures du même coup d'archet en *f*
b) par 4 mesures du même coup d'archet en *p*
c) par 8 mesures du même coup d'archet en *ppp*

*Cvičení v táhlých tonech a v zadržovaném smyku.*
*Předchozí cvičení čís. 3 - 7 a 13 - 17 cvič následovně:*

*a) po 2 taktech jedním smykem f*
*b) po 4 taktech jedním smykem p*
*c) po 8 taktech jedním smykem ppp*

Exercise in sustained tones and in economising the bow-length, i.e. holding it back as much as possible.
Practice the preceding exercises № 3 to 7 and 13 to 17 in the following styles of bowing, namely:

a) in groups of 2 bars to one stroke of the bow *f*
b) in groups of 4 bars to one stroke of the bow *p*
c) in groups of 8 bars to one stroke of the bow *ppp*

Упражненіе въ протяжныхъ тонахъ и въ задерживаніи смычка.
Предыдущіе этюды NN№ 3 – 7 и 13 – 17 должно исполнять, связывая такты слѣдующими способами:

а) по 2 такта подъ одинъ смычокъ въ *f*
б) по 4 такта подъ одинъ смычокъ въ *p*
в) по 8 тактовъ подъ одинъ смычокъ въ *ppp*

Uebungen in gebrochenen Akkorden auf 3 und 4 Saiten mit Anwendung der vorhergehenden Stricharten.

Exercices en accords brisés sur 3 et 4 cordes en appliquant les coups d'archet précédents. —
*Cvičení v lomených akkordech na 3 a 4 strunách podlé předchozích smykových cvičení.*

Exercises in arpeggios (broken, harp-like chords) across 3 and 4 strings, us-ing the preceding styles of bowing.

Упражненія ломанными аккордами на 3 и 4 струнахъ съ примѣненіемъ предыдущихъ движеній смычка.

# № 21.

Mit Stricharten 1–97 aus № 13.

Avec les coups d'archet 1–97 du №13. *Smyky 1-97 z čis. 13.*

With the styles of bowing prescribed in Nos 1 to 97 of № 13.
Движеніями смычка 1–97 изъ № 13.

# № 22.

Mit Stricharten aus № 16.

Avec les coups d'archet № 16. *Smyky z čis. 16.*

With the bowings shown in № 16.
Движеніями смычка изъ № 16.

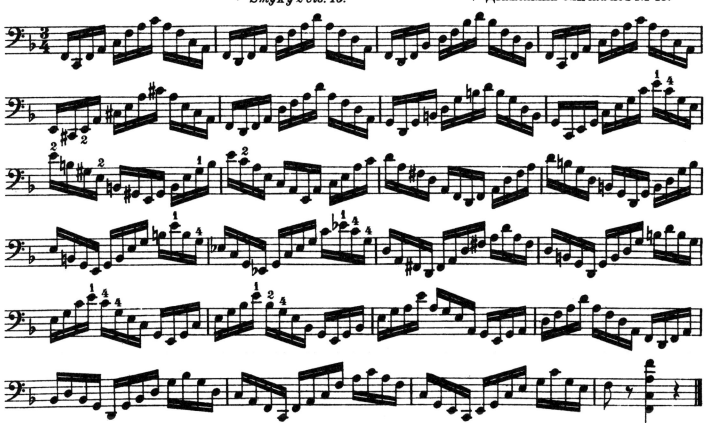

# № 23.

Mit Stricharten aus № 17.

Avec les coups d'archet du № 17
*Smyky z čís.17.*

With the bowings shown in № 17.
Движеніями смычка изъ № 17.

# № 24.

Mit Stricharten aus № 15.

Avec les coups d'archet du № 15.
*Smyky z čís.15.*

With the bowings shown in № 15.
Движеніями смычка изъ № 15.

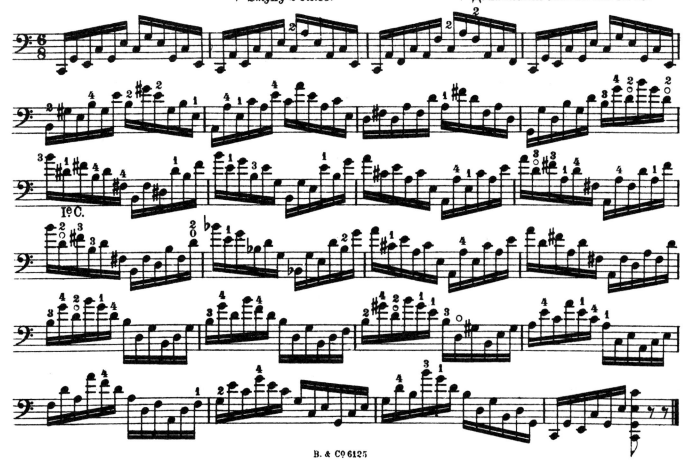

B. & C⁰ 6125

Anwendung der vorhergehenden Strich-arten auf hohen Lagen.

Emploi des coups d'archet précédents dans les positions élevées.

*Dle předešlých cvičení smykových ve vyso-kých polohách.*

Utilisation of the preceding bowing - styles in the high Positions.

Примѣненiе предыдущихъ движенiй смычка на высокихъ позицiяхъ.

# № 25.

Mit Stricharten aus № 14.

Avec les coups d'archet du № 14.
*Smyky z čís. 14.*

With the bowing-styles of № 14.
Движенiями смычка изъ № 14.

Diese Übung kann ganz in der Daumenlage ge-spielt werden.

Cet exercice peut se jouer entièrement à la position du pouce.
*Celéto to cvičení lze hráti v poloze palcové.*

This exercise may be played entirely in the Position of the Thumb.

Это упражненiе можно играть все въ по-зицiи большого пальца.

# № 26.

Mit Stricharten aus № 13.

Avec les coups d'archet du № 13.
*Smyky z čís. 13.*

With the bowing-styles prescribed in №13.
Движенiями смычка изъ № 13.

*) Daumenlage.
*) *Position du pouce.*
*) Position of the Thumb.

*) *Poloha palcová.*

*) Позицiя большого пальца.

*) Der Daumen darf während der ganzen Übung seinen Platz nicht verändern.
*) Le pouce ne doit pas changer de place pendant tout l'exercice.
*) The thumb must not change its place during the whole exercise.

*) Palec nemění po celé cvičení svoji polohu

B. & C° 6125

*) Большой палецъ не долженъ мѣнять свое положенiе въ теченiе цѣлаго упражненiя.

# № 27.

Mit Stricharten aus № 15.

Avec les coups d'archet du № 15
*Smyky z čís. 15*

With the bowing-styles prescribed in № 15.
Движеніями смычка изъ № 15.

Daumenlage.
*Position du pouce.*
Position of the Thumb.

*Poloha palcová.*
Положеніе большого
пальца.

# № 28.

Mit Stricharten aus № 17.

Avec les coups d'archet du № 17.
*Smyky z čís. 17.*

With the bowing-styles prescribed in № 17.
Движеніями смычка изъ № 17.

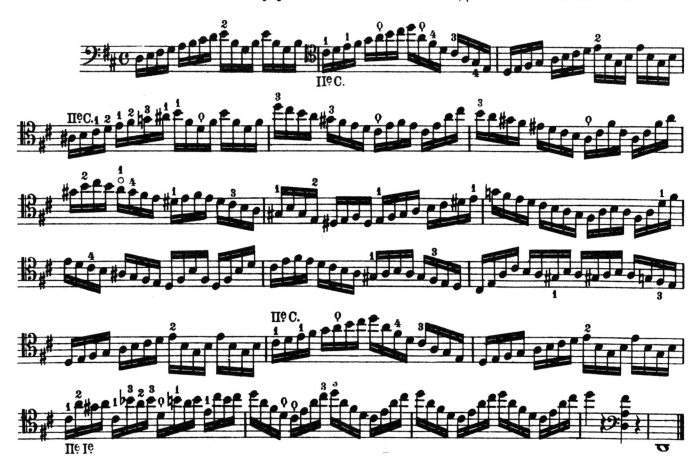